IMAGES OF WA

SS DAS REICH AT WAR 1939-45

RARE PHOTOGRAPHS FROM WARTIME ARCHIVES

Ian Baxter

Pen & Sword
MILITARY

First published in Great Britain in 2017 by
PEN & SWORD MILITARY
An imprint of
Pen & Sword Books Ltd
47 Church Street
Barnsley
South Yorkshire
S70 2AS

ISBN 978-1-47389-089-3

Typeset by Concept, Huddersfield, West Yorkshire HD4 5JL.
Printed and bound in England by CPI Group (UK) Ltd, Croydon CR0 4YY.

Pen & Sword Books Ltd incorporates the imprints of Pen & Sword Archaeology, Atlas, Aviation, Battleground, Discovery, Family History, History, Maritime, Military, Naval, Politics, Railways, Select, Social History, Transport, True Crime, and Claymore Press, Frontline Books, Leo Cooper, Praetorian Press, Remember When, Seaforth Publishing and Wharncliffe.

For a complete list of Pen & Sword titles please contact
PEN & SWORD BOOKS LIMITED
47 Church Street, Barnsley, South Yorkshire S70 2AS, England
E-mail: enquiries@pen-and-sword.co.uk
Website: www.pen-and-sword.co.uk

Contents

Introduction

Between 1933 and 1939, the power of the SS grew considerably, with thousands of men being recruited into the new ideological elite armed formation, many of them into units known as the SS-Verfügungstruppe (Special Disposal Troop). These SS-VT troops first saw blood in Poland and then in 1940 on the Western Front. Out of this new formation the SS Das Reich Division was born.

This book contains over 250 rare and unpublished photographs, with text and captions which describe the fighting tactics, the uniforms, the battles and the different elements that went into making the Das Reich Division such an elite fighting force. It describes how it evolved, how it battled its way through Poland, the Low Countries, the Balkans and the Eastern Front, and then in the last year how it defended Normandy and then Germany to the end. It reveals how it fought and was forced to withdraw under overwhelming enemy superiority. It shows how it was rushed from one danger zone to another to plug gaps in the front wherever they appeared. Often they fought and won against enemies ten times their strength and were thereby both feared and revered. This book is a unique glimpse into one of the most famous fighting machines of the Second World War and a great addition to the library of any reader interested in Waffen-SS history.

Chapter One

Training

D as Reich's origins dated back to 1933 when the Standarte 'Deutschland' division was created. A year later a second division was formed, known as 'Germania', and in March 1938 a third and final Standarte was created in Vienna, known as the 'Der Führer'. In 1936 both 'Deutschland' and Germania' were expanded to regimental size with three battalions each. These battalions became known as the SS-VT or SS-Verfügungstruppe (Special Disposal Troop). In 1939 'Der Führer' became part of the SS-VT.

Training the SS-VT battalions for war was of the utmost importance to Hitler. Its men initially had to depend on the Wehrmacht for weapons and training, but later Himmler established SS-Junkerschule Bad Tölz and SS-Junkerschule Braunschweig for training of SS officers.

Himmler set strict requirements for the recruits. They had to be German nationals who could prove their Aryan ancestry back to 1800, have no criminal record, and be unmarried. Each recruit was committed to four years in the SS-VT. They had to be between the ages of 17 and 23 and be at least 1.74 metres (5 feet 9 inches) in height. They had to have no dental fillings, have 20/20 eyesight, and provide medical certification.

By 1938 some of the recruitment restrictions had been relaxed, including the minimum height, the dental fillings and the 20/20 vision.

Inspector of the SS-VT was Brigadeführer Paul Hausser, who worked tirelessly in the late 1930s to transform the SS-VT into a superior killing machine. Training was often gruelling and the men had to serve Hausser with allegiance and fanaticism. Promotions within the SS-VT cadre were common, and this gave the men an insight into the running of the organisation. They were taught about inferior races and enemies of the state, such as Jews and Bolsheviks, for whom they were to show no mercy. Only the toughest and most determined men were of any use to Hausser.

By the late 1930s Nazi foreign policy became increasingly aggressive. Hausser made it clear to his men that they were to prepare for war. New slogans of hatred and discrimination were plastered around the barracks for the men to read.

Now well-trained and fanatically indoctrinated, the men of the SS-VT were ready for their baptism of fire.

A posed photograph showing new recruits at their training barracks. In 1939 the SS-VT were posted at their home stations of Würzburg, Erlangen, Ahlen, Münster and Westphalia.

Three photographs showing an SS-VT regimental band marching probably during a passing out parade at a training barracks.

(**Above**) A commanding officer speaks to recruits on the main square of the unit's barracks. Note how new the SS garrison appears. All the officers have armbands, probably with the inscription 'Germania' printed on them.

(**Opposite, above**) Two soldiers pause during training. They stand with one of the divisional heavy armoured cars, the eight-wheeled Sd.Kfz.231 armed with a 2cm gun for local defence. These vehicles were employed in one heavy platoon. Note the inscription 'Derfflinger' painted in white on the vehicle. This was a famous German Field Marshal called Georg von Derfflinger who fought in the Thirty Years' War with distinction against the Swedes.

(**Opposite, below**) Commanding officers can be seen with their men at a training barracks in the summer of 1939. While training for the new recruits was often tough and required great stamina both physically and mentally, the men knew that they were to become a fighting elite.

(**Above**) SS-VT troops during a parade. Some of the men are armed with the standard German army bolt action rifle, the Karabiner 98K. This weapon would also be the standard armament for the Waffen-SS during the war.

(**Opposite, above**) A group photograph of an SS-VT regiment at one the training camps.

(**Opposite, below**) Here we have an excellent view of the Das Reich training barracks, including garages and square, used primarily for exercises of the kitchen and bakery staff. Note the different camouflage pattern of tents used. These were standard issue Wehrmacht equipment.

(**Above**) Commanding officers' area seen during a parade at one of the training grounds in mid-1939. The commanders put much emphasis on their men to be brutal and unsympathetic to their foes. Their training was one of the main reasons for their cruelty both on and off the battlefield.

(**Opposite, above**) During a training exercise and live ammunition is being used on the training grounds. Using live ammunition was another way the men were hardened and taught not be afraid.

(**Opposite, above**) At their home station and local men, women and children watch newly recruited men of Germania during a ceremony. These SS-VT units comprised three regiments known as Deutschland, Germania and Der Führer. They typically had a strength of three battalions.

Five photographs showing soldiers of the Germania battalion during guard duties at their home station in the early summer of 1939.

Soldiers belonging to Germania during a winter exercise in early 1939. Note how the men are marching with little protection against the weather. This photo is quite striking as most of the soldiers that fought during the onset of the winter campaign in Russia in 1941 were wearing similar clothing.

Under the watchful eye of their trainers, men of the SS-VT are put through their paces marching around the barracks. The men are all wearing their summer uniforms, but with winter gloves. During the winter, since 1937, the men were issued with a woolen waistcoat or a sweater to wear under their uniform.

A motorcycle rider complete with sidecar combination poses for the camera on his BMW. Note full tactical markings painted either in yellow or white on the front of the sidecar. This indicates it belongs to a bakery company and the 3rd vehicle in that company. Note the Opel Blitz truck stationary in the background with number 4 painted in white on the side.

Chapter Two

Baptism of Fire
(1939–41)

For the invasion of Poland, SS-VT units and other German forces mobilised and took up their positions in preparation for attack. They comprised three regiments known as Deutschland, Germania and Der Führer. They had a typical strength of three battalions.

Tasked to attack out of East Prussia was Panzer-Division Kempf, named after its commander Major General Werner Kempf. This division was in the 1st Corps of the 3rd Army. The infantry regiment attached to Division-Kempf was the Deutschland Regiment. The Germania Regiment, the Leibstandarte SS Adolf Hitler (LSSAH) and other SS forces served in areas further south. The Germania Regiment was attached to various sections of the 14th Army, while the Der Führer Regiment remained in the Black Forest still on training and recruiting duties.

During the early hours of 1 September 1939 the 3rd Army attacked out of East Prussia into Poland to achieve its first tactical objectives; its main strategic objective was to reach Warsaw. Its forces were soon met by strong and determined resistance and the Deutschland Regiment fought a number of hard-pressed battles against a network of well-entrenched fortifications.

Simultaneously, in the south of the country, the Germania Regiment and other units of the 10th and 14th Armies pushed eastwards towards the San River. Within hours of the German attack, bewildered Polish commanders struggled despairingly to hold their forces together. In many areas the virtual collapse of the communication system left many commands isolated and unable to establish contact with the fronts. Consequently decisions were almost invariably late and disastrously overtaken by events with the result that one position after another was lost to the Germans. Already the fleeing Polish Army were being mauled almost to death by constant air attacks and pounded mercilessly by tanks and artillery.

In the eyes of the SS-VT, this new type of warfare was exactly what these troops had trained for. It was not like the dehumanizing years of trench warfare in the 1914–18 war, but Blitzkrieg, a swift all-out attack of such ferocity that victory would be secured quickly and decisively. The Poles were faced with the finest fighting army the world had ever seen. Their tactics were the best: stubborn defence; concentrated local firepower from machine-guns and mortars; rapid counter-attacks to recover lost ground. Units fought on even when cut off.

The SS-VT had shown its worth in the first Blitzkrieg operation of the Second World War. It had fought with zeal and with devastating effect against its demoralised foe. The German march through Poland took no more than eighteen days to achieve. By this time the Germans had moreover swept every Polish division clean off the map, brought thundering Panzer divisions to the far corners of eastern Poland and outflanked and outmanoeuvred its opponents with skill, verging on brilliance. The days that followed consisted of a series of actions against the last remnants of the Polish Army.

Following the crushing of Poland in early October 1939 the number of SS-VT forces were increased to some 100,000 troops, and put under the command of Paul Hausser.

By April 1940 the SS-VT received more support units and fresh troops. It was organized into three regimental units, each of them comprising three battalions with three infantry companies and one heavy company. With this strengthened organization it was deemed more than ready to participate in the planned invasion of the Low Countries. Moreover, the men were highly motivated to perform their duty to the 'Fatherland' and use their skill and tenacity on the battlefield with overwhelming results. The men had bonded well over the past months since the Polish campaign and developed a strong sense of comradeship and loyalty to their divisional commander, whom they affectionately called 'Papa' Hauser.

Thus, when the German Army crossed over into the Low Countries in May 1940, the SS-VT, with all its energy and resolve, were unwavering to win another victory, this time on the Western Front. Under the powerful arm of the German 18th Army, the Der Führer Regiment, the 2nd Battalion of the division's artillery regiment, a pioneer company, and a vehicle column attached to the 207th Infantry Division, unleashed its might across the Dutch frontier. Flanking the 2nd Battalion was the division's reconnaissance detachment and the Deutschland Regiment's armoured car platoon, which served with the 254th Infantry Division. Almost immediately the Der Führer Regiment became heavily embroiled in fighting as it carved its way through the weak Dutch front lines. Behind it the remainder of the SS-VT waited impatiently to have its baptism of fire while forward echelons of the 207th Infantry Division pushed through deeper into Holland.

Across the whole front the Dutch defence soon crumbled. Through the retreating column that littered almost every main road, Dutch troops outnumbered the exodus of refugees. Most of the Dutch artillery was pulled by horses or mules, and the wounded were carried on carts. The picture was one of a defeated army trying in vain to escape the impending slaughter.

Elsewhere along the front lines the situation was equally as grim. Dutch troops had tried to hold their meager positions against overwhelming forces but were systematically battered into submission by the German Blitzkrieg tactics.

The SS advanced alongside their Wehrmacht counterparts and it did not take long for them to penetrate deep into enemy lines. Across the front SS troops were seen leading furious attacks on the bewildered Dutch troops, soon occupying the eastern end of Fortress Holland. 10 Corps swept past Utrecht and into the Dutch capital, Amsterdam. Although the Der Führer Regiment had achieved noticeable success for its actions in Holland, the rest of the SS-Verfügungs Division did not see as much action in the country. During the early phase of the attack the main body of the division advanced in two motorized columns to Hivarenbeck, north of Antwerp. Yet in spite of a slow start the SS-Verfügungs Division soon secured German control over the western end of Holland. Wehrmacht troops of Heeresgruppe B moved across into Belgium, captured Brussels, swept through Belgium and into northern France, and then moved towards the English Channel.

On the evening of 22 May, the SS-Verfügungs Division drove with the 6th and 8th Panzer Divisions towards the port of Calais in order to help strengthen German positions west and south of the Dunkirk perimeter. However, within sight of encircling and destroying British and French forces in Dunkirk, on the night of 26 May Hitler rescinded his famous 'halt order' and Germania and Der Führer of the SS-Verfügungs Division withdrew and took up positions against enemy forces in the Nieppe Forest. As for the Deutschland Regiment it was temporarily attached to the 3rd Panzer Division, and became embroiled in heavy fighting against British units on the Lys Canal near Merville.

With the first phase of the battle in the west won, the Germans began their second phase, the attack on France. As the main body of the German Army attacked on 5 June 1940, SS formations had already arrived on the outskirts of Paris. The French capital had been abandoned by its government. Panzergruppe Kleist, including the Totenkopf, LSSAH and the SS-VT Division, struck through Champagne toward Dijon in Burgundy to prevent the remnants of the French Army retreating to the south-west of France.

By 25 June 1940, the day on which the ceasefire went into effect, the Totenkopf and SS-Verfügungs Division were near Bordeaux, preparing to occupy the coastal sector.

It was estimated that by this time some 500,000 French soldiers had been captured. Large amounts of battlefield booty too fell into German hands. To make the problems even greater for the French the Italians had declared war on France sending some thirty-two divisions against some six French divisions. However, against 185,000 troops the Italians made little progress against well-trained French soldiers of the Alps.

In total some 94,000 French soldiers had been killed in the battle for France and about 250,000 injured. Almost 2 million French soldiers were taken prisoner by the Germans. By contrast, the German losses were much less, with 27,000 dead and 111,000 wounded.

The battle of France had ended with another decisive victory for the Germans. They had reaped the fruits of another dramatic Blitzkrieg campaign. France had proven to be ideal tank country in which to undertake a lightening war, and its conception seemed flawless. To many of the tacticians Blitzkrieg would ensure future victories.

As for the men of the SS-Verfügungs Division they had fought with skill and tenacity, and following the victory over France, many soldiers and their commanders received accolades for their bravery and leadership in the field.

In late 1940 the SS-Verfügungs Division returned to southern France and was stationed at the town of Vsoul. In December the division was reorganized. The Germania Regiment was removed from the Verfügungs-Division and used to form the main part of a new division, SS-Division Germania. This unit was made up mostly of Nordic volunteers from the newly conquered territories, Dutch, Flemings, Danes, and Norwegians.

In December 1940, the Verfügungs Division was renamed the SS Deutschland Division, and then a few weeks later the SS Reich Division (Motorized). The division's strength was increased and it received its divisional insignia of the Wolfsangel. As for Germania, this was renamed Wiking.

By March 1941 the SS Reich Division was combat-ready and was transported from southern France to south-west Romania where it had orders to attack Yugoslavia with the sole objective to capture the capital, Belgrade. In April 1941, the German invasion of Yugoslavia and Greece was initiated. The LSSAH and Das Reich were attached to separate army Panzer corps. Fritz Klingenberg, a company commander in the Das Reich, led his men across Yugoslavia to Belgrade, where SS Reich Division was given the honour of leading the charge. By this time there was little opposition and the city was captured with few casualties.

Following the quick victory in Yugoslavia the SS Reich Division returned to Romania and later moved to an area near Salzburg, Austria, for a rest and refit. During this period the division was reorganized. It consisted of the two SS regiments, Der Führer and Deutschland, and upgraded to three strong battalions of motorized infantry, comprising a battery of artillery, platoons of motorcycle rifles, and armoured cars. The division had a strong artillery regiment that consisted of four battalions (standard was three) with three companies in each of them.

By mid-June the SS Reich Division was transported to Poland and ordered to take up positions near the River Bug for military preparations against the Soviet Union.

The campaigns on the Western Front and in Yugoslavia which had brought death and destruction to their foes had made the SS Reich Division almost invincible. They had consistently performed with tenacity and won the confidence and gratitude of their beloved Führer. However the campaign on the Eastern Front would be like no other conflict they had ever experienced.

Infantrymen marching through Holland in May 1940. During the initial stages of the invasion of Holland, SS-VT units operated separately under the command of 18th Army. Its main objective was to reach Rotterdam by first punching a hole through the Ijssel and Maas rivers at the cities of Arnhem, Nijmegen and Malden, near the German border.

During the opening phases of the campaign on the Western Front a group of soldiers belonging to the Der Führer Regiment pause during fighting among some buildings. Note their collar patches, indicating they belong to the 3rd Regiment of the Das Reich division.

(**Opposite page**) An infantryman pauses in his march. Within days the SS-VT units had secured a number of towns in Holland. By 12 May 1940, the Der Führer Regiment was given the honour of spearheading the main German assault on the eastern line of Fortress Holland. This area was regarded as a very significant obstacle standing between the Germans and the old capital of the Netherlands. Der Führer made an aggressive attack, quickly occupied the eastern end of Fortress Holland, and swept past Utrecht into Amsterdam.

(**This page**) Three photographs showing a Das Reich motorcycle reconnaissance platoon travelling along a road. These men belong to the 2nd Regiment Germania. A typical motorcycle reconnaissance platoon comprised ten motorcycles including sidecar combinations.

(**Opposite, above**) Another photograph showing a Das Reich motorcycle reconnaissance platoon.

(**Opposite, below**) A Horch heavy car Kfz 4 of a reconnaissance battalion advances along a road. For aerial recognition purposes, the German national flag was often draped across vehicles in the early part of the war.

(**Above, left**) A heavy weapon platoon during the early phase of fighting on the Western Front. One of the soldiers, of an anti-tank rifle section, is armed with a PzB 39.

(**Above, right**) Staff and line officers from an infantry and motorcycle troop survey maps prior to further operations in the field.

Another photograph showing staff and line officers from an infantry and motorcycle troop surveying maps prior to further operations in the field.

On the march along one of the many canals that covered Holland and Belgium a soldier can be seen armed with a PzB 39. He is accompanied by an NCO.

Soldiers of a heavy MG platoon during a march. They can clearly be seen carrying their equipment, consisting of MG34 tripod and ammunition boxes. They are armed with the standard Karabiner 98K bolt action rifle. Note that the men are newly recruited into the ranks of the SS-VT as they still have no SS collar patches.

A great photograph showing a heavy MG34 machine gun section. The weapon has been mounted on a tripod. Note the soldier equipped with a small rangefinder which was used for correcting fire at longer ranges.

More than likely at a forward observation post and NCOs belonging to Deutschland survey the terrain for the enemy through a pair of 6 × 30 Zeiss binoculars.

Along a road is a heavy MG platoon. The infantry battalion's machine gun company had two heavy machine gun platoons, each with four guns. Each infantry battalion contained an MG company which fielded eight MG34 heavy machine guns on the sustained-fire mount. At the sides of roads or in open terrain they would protect the flanks of advancing rifle companies, as in this photograph.

(**Opposite, above**) A heavy MG34 team preparing their weapon for action. Note the tube for two spare barrels. In open terrain the MG34 machine gun squad would use their sustained-fire mount to protect the flanks of advancing rifle companies. In built-up areas the crews often had to operate forward with the rifle platoons and in light machine gun roles with bipods only. They were still able sometimes to take advantage of the situation and revert back to a heavy machine gun role.

(**Opposite, below**) A heavy MG34 troop belonging to a motorcycle unit is seen entering a village. A heavy machine gun troop was provided with a tripod mount (Lafette 34) with a pair of leather carrying slings (Trageriemen), a long-range optical sight (Zieleinrichtung 34), at least two spare barrel carriers (Laufbehalter 34), a belt-filling device (Gurtfüller 34) and a number of 300-round metal cartridge cases, plus various items of cleaning equipment.

(**Above**) A Pak 35/36 anti-tank gun crew of the 2nd SS Regiment Germania moving their weapon into position. The Pak 35/36 emerged in 1939 as the first anti-tank weapon to serve both the Heer and Waffen-SS.

A motorcycle pioneer platoon can be seen removing mines from a road. Note the soldier in the background equipped with mine detector.

(**Opposite, above**) Another photograph showing a Pak 35/36 anti-tank gun crew. By the time it saw its debut on the Eastern Front a year later the German gunners soon realized how limited the weapon was in an anti-tank capability.

(**Opposite, below**) A photograph taken the moment a 10.5cm le.FH18 howitzer is fired against an enemy target. The 10.5cm howitzer had a nine-man crew. Usually fewer are seen serving this piece because often some of the crew were to the rear with the horses, limber and caisson.

A light MG34 machine gun crew on the march through a field during operations on the Western Front in 1940. The machine gunner is carrying his weapon at the ready.

A group of soldiers on the move through a captured village. The equipment worn by these infantrymen could carry enough to sustain them for several days. Note the rifleman on the right; he has ammunition pouches for his Kar 98k bolt action rifle that he is holding, a gas mask cape, an entrenching tool and a pair of Zeiss binoculars.

An assault troop being carried to the forward edge of the battlefield in a Horch Kfz 4 heavy car. Of interest is that a number of the infantrymen have smeared mud over their helmets in order to conceal them in undergrowth.

The crew of a PaK35/36 during an enemy contact. This weapon was the standard anti-tank gun of the Landser during the early part of the war. It weighed only 432kg and had sloping splinter shield. The gun fired a solid shot round at a muzzle velocity of 2,500 feet per second to a maximum range of 4,000 metres.

Nur keinen Laut!

(**Opposite page**) Three photographs showing 'Germania' infantry with their Obersturmführer commanding officer. The men are preparing go into action. One of the soldiers is a medical orderly and can be seen with a white armband with red cross. He is equipped with special pouches and his MG34 ammunition boxes have been used for storing dressing materials. Note the soldier carrying a Dreifuss M34 anti-aircraft tripod.

(**Above**) Infantry take cover. A column of Pz.Kpfw.IIs can be seen stationary at the side of the road. Leading the column is a Pz.Kpfw.I. Both in Poland and on the Western Front the success of the Blitzkrieg strategy of warfare owed much to the German light tanks, in spite of them being intended primarily for training and light reconnaissance work.

During a lull in the fighting and infantrymen can be seen sitting next to a road. For armament they carry the Mauser 7.9mm Kar98k carbine, the standard army issue shoulder weapon. One soldier, probably a troop leader, is armed with the MP38/40 machine pistol.

An NCO from the Germania Regiment. Typically for this unit, he has rank insignia on shoulder straps and collar, but has no SS collar patches.

Heavily loaded soldiers of an infantry platoon crossing a stream during May 1940. They are armed with the usual rifleman's equipment: the enlisted man's SS leather belt, M1939 infantry leather support straps, rifle ammunition pouches, bread bag, field flask with drinking cup, mess kit, shelter quarters, and gasmask in its M1938 metal canister.

(**Opposite page**) Pioneer troops being directed by their squad leader, who is armed with an MP40 sub-machine gun. He wears the usual NCO's equipment; of note he wears what appears to be the 1st pattern MP39/40 magazine pouch. Two stick grenades are tucked into his black leather belt.

(**Above**) Troops pause during their march across France in 1940. The NCO can be seen with a piece of paper and is referring to this before commencing movement. Behind his troop are other soldiers paused in a field awaiting the order to move.

(**Opposite page**) Infantrymen are preparing to commence their march across France. The men are all armed with 7.92mm Mauser Kar98k carbine. This bolt-action rifle had a five-round magazine and soldiers typically carried sixty rounds in two three-pocket leather cartridge pouches on their front belt, as in this photograph.

(**Above**) Men of a Germania MG troop are seen here being led by their NCO, who is armed with an MP35. Hanging around his neck on his chest is the magazine pouch. Behind him is an ammunition carrier with a MG34 75-round belt slung around his neck.

Three photographs showing soldiers of the Deutschland regiment with a 6-metre inflatable boat for a river crossing operation. Two paddles either side was normally sufficient enough for the boat to be propelled through the water, even when carrying a full complement of infantry onboard with heavy weapons and equipment. A number of heavy pieces of equipment could also be loaded on these boats, which included the 8cm mortar, 2cm anti-aircraft gun and 7.5cm infantry gun.

(**Opposite, above**) Soldiers of the Deutschland regiment in a river crossing operation.

(**Opposite, below**) During an attack along a river bank and a platoon is marching in a column towards enemy positions under direct cover from MG and mortar fire.

(**Above**) From a dug-in position infantrymen pause in their advance. Note the Mauser C96 (Konstruktion 96) semi-automatic pistol sited on the top of their position.

(**Opposite, above**) An injured infantryman is being transported back to the rear to be treated for his wounds. His stretcher has been secured on a BMW motorcycle combination.

(**Above, left**) Another mode of transport popular with the Heer throughout the war was the bicycle. In Holland and France, where the terrain was often flat, troops often used bicycles to get from one part of the front to another.

(**Opposite, below**) 'Das Reich' troops being transported onboard a Kfz 4 Horch heavy car. They are ready at a moment's notice to jump off the vehicle and go into action.

(**Above, right**) A machine gunner racing to another position with his light MG being used from its bipod mount. With the bipod extended and the belt loaded, the machine gunner could effectively move the weapon quickly from one position to another, throw it to the ground and put it into operation with deadly effect.

(**Opposite, above**) A platoon of SS soldiers travelling through a destroyed French town in a column of Opel Blitz infantry light trucks. Each vehicle carried a squad of twelve men with all their kit and additional equipment. Note the vehicle with the number 7 painted in white on the rear. This indicates the vehicle's position within the company.

(**Opposite, below**) A motorcyclist giving a signal as he passes a column. Motorcyclists could be found in every unit of an infantry and Panzer division, especially during the early part of the war. They were also incorporated in the divisional staffs, which included a motorcycle messenger platoon.

(**Above**) Photographed from a staff vehicle, an officer can be seen acknowledging a supporting motorcyclist as they move along a road. The motorcyclist is wearing a rubberized motorcycle coat, aviator goggles, as well as personal equipment.

A motorcyclist pauses in his march and sleeps next to his bike. He is wearing the motorcycle coat. All motorcycle units and individual motorcyclists, regardless of rank, were issued with the loose-fitting, rubberized coat. The tail of the coat could be gathered in around the wearer's legs and buttoned down.

During a stop in the advance this motorcycle troop, attached to the SS 2nd Regiment Germania, tuck into some of their rations.

A mortar crew with their 5cm IGrW 36 mortar. It was common for infantry, especially during long, intensive periods of action, to fire their mortar from either trenches or dug-in positions where the mortar crew could be protected from enemy fire.

An SS soldier can be seen milking a cow in order to put some variety into his comrade's daily rations.

It appears that these NCOs are writing orders for their men. All over the front the Germans were penetrating British and French lines sending them reeling back towards the Channel coast.

An SS column passes a long line of French PoWs being led along a road back to the rear.

Soldiers belonging to Germania on the march. Note the MG34 slung over the machine gunner's shoulder.

(**Opposite, above**) An SS motorcycle unit pose for the camera in France. All the men are wearing the standard army greatcoat.

(**Opposite, below & above**) Two photographs showing long columns of dejected French PoWs being led away to the rear. In early June 1940 both the BEF and French forces were being rapidly crushed by overwhelming German forces.

More French PoWs being led away to the rear.

Moroccan and French troops being led away as PoWs. Moroccan forces fought fiercely against Waffen-SS units in late May 1940. Most surrendering Africans were simply shot out of hand, being considered 'sub-humans' by the SS.

British PoWs with a Das Reich unit in a wooded clearing in late May 1940. An officer is tending to an injured soldier.

The devastation wrought on French and BEF columns in northern France was extensive. They were subject to constant ground and aerial attacks as they withdrew ahead of the rapidly moving German armoured spearheads. Carnage of dead horses and abandoned carts and weapons littered the roads and lanes.

One of the many captured French bunker systems that were built as defensive positions. This bunker has seen much shelling and gun fire.

An interesting photograph showing a long column of Das Reich vehicles in northern France during the famous Hitler 'halt order'. On the night of 26 May 1940, the 'halt order' was rescinded and the Germania and Der Führer regiments surged back into action to fight a bloody battle in the Nieppe Forest. The remaining infantry regiment, Deutschland, which was temporarily attached to the 3rd Panzer Division, took part in the attack against British units on the Lys Canal near Merville.

Here the MG34 gunner is using his machine gun in an anti-aircraft role, which on the battlefield would be quite successful against low-flying enemy targets. The MG34, on its sustained mount in an AA role, was more than capable of damaging or bringing down an aircraft.

A prime mover towing a 10.5cm le.FH18 howitzer across a pontoon bridge. The 10.5cm howitzer had a nine-man crew. More than 5,000 of these light field howitzers entered service when the war broke out and remained the standard light divisional howitzer throughout the war.

(**Opposite, above**) A battery of 10.5cm le.FH18 howitzers in a French field. A gun crew stand around preparing their position for action. Ammunition handlers can be seen standing with ammunition and propellant charges stacked before loading the gun. The 10.5cm light infantry gun provided the division with a versatile, mobile base of fire. While it was not very effective against heavily defended concrete emplacements, it was successful against more lightly defended positions.

(**Opposite, below**) From the roadside an SS infantryman takes a photograph of the endless stream of refugees pouring westwards and southwards through France. One of the biggest problems faced by German logistics was the number of refugees jamming the already congested roads.

(**Above**) Supply vehicles cross a pontoon bridge. Because of the large numbers of rivers and streams encountered during the advance all kinds of bridging and river crossings were essential if the Germans were successfully to achieve their objectives.

Two photographs taken in sequence showing an SS soldier ridiculing the British for their failure on the Western Front. The soldier insults his foe by wearing a bowler hat and riding a donkey.

SS troops stand at the base of the Eiffel Tower following the capture of the French capital. Paris fell on 14 June 1940. Two days later German troops went on a victory parade through the city. A week later France surrendered and, for the men of the SS, the campaign in the west was over.

Three photographs showing graves of Das Reich soldiers following the end of the campaign in the west in 1940. Casualty rates were higher than predicted in the SS-VT because they were often at the forefront of the battle. In spite of the losses, the campaign was for the SS a complete success.

Troops transferring from train to road. These Das Reich troops are unloading essential equipment from flatbed railways cars at Timişoara in Romania ready for the long hard journey by road. This SS unit had already been on the move for a week, having travelled from southern France to western Romania by rail.

A column of Das Reich troops on horseback on the march towards Belgrade. Both the LSSAH and Das Reich were attached to separate army Panzer Corps. Fritz Klingenberg, a company commander in Das Reich, led his men across Yugoslavia to the capital, Belgrade, where SS Das Reich Division was given the honour of leading the charge into Belgrade.

A Horch cross-country vehicle attached to Das Reich is seen during the Balkans campaign. Note the tactical symbol painted in white on the front left mudguard. Most German military vehicles carried symbols to denote the unit to which they were assigned. These tactical symbols were modified from German military map symbols for various types of weapons and vehicles, and were mainly applied in white.

A train carrying supplies to the Balkan front has halted on a main line, and troops are being handed out rations from a supply truck onboard the flatbed railway car.

Chapter Three

Victories on the Eastern Front (1941–42)

During the early morning of 22 June 1941, the German Army finally unleashed the maelstrom that was Barbarossa. Both the infantry and panzer divisions wasted no time and soon sliced through the bewildered Russian forces on every front. The ferocity and effectiveness of both the infantry and panzer divisions were so great that some of the Red Army forces they surrounded were gigantic. Groups of up to fifteen Russian divisions were trapped at a time and systematically annihilated in a hurricane of fire.

As for the Das Reich Division, it moved across the frontier to begin operations. Das Reich was incorporated into 46th Panzer Corps along with 10th Panzer Division and the famous Großdeutschland Division on the central sector of the Eastern Front. It was ordered to push its forces in the direction of the Białystok region where it clashed with Soviet forces.

Das Reich's advance went well and within a few weeks it arrived in the area around Yelnia, where leading spearheads of Army Group Centre had slowed. Das Reich, along with other Corps units, then fought a series of heavy battles around Yelnia where it struggled to stem strong and determined Soviet forces. In spite of serious ammunition shortages, the SS units were successful and forced badly mauled Russian troops to finally abandon Yelnia. However, it was not without serious loss in men and equipment, although Soviet losses were much higher.

Following fighting around Yelnia, Das Reich was pulled out of the area after receiving quite a heavy mauling. It was moved into the rear areas where the division recuperated and re-strengthened its force. By the time it was battle ready, the Wehrmacht had penetrated quite deeply into Russian territory, and it looked as though Das Reich were going to play a lighter role in the last phase of what they thought would be the defeat of the Soviet Union.

In southern Russia the German war machine had already opened up the front. The main thrust was directed between the southern edge of the Pripet Marshes and the foothills of the Carpathian Mountains. It seemed that the German success in the south had completely mastered the enemy, despite being continually harassed by

Russian forces that had been cut off in the wooded swampland between the Pripet Marshes and the Carpathians. The Wehrmacht were determined to push on towards the Dnieper River, as its primary task was to hold onto as much ground as possible and prevent all intact retreating enemy formations from withdrawing deep into Russia. By August the Wehrmacht had swung out east of Kiev and began mopping up the last remnants in and around the besieged city. To annihilate the last remaining resistance the 2nd Army and 2nd Panzer Group were to sweep in from the north and take up blocking positions east of the city. Moving up from the south the 17th Army and 1st Panzer Troop were to advance on to the outskirts of the city and link up with the other two German formations, with the main plan of preventing the Soviets from escaping to the east. Attached to 2nd Panzer Group was the Das Reich Division.

The plan to prevent the escape of the Russian forces trapped in Kiev was a complete success, and when the battle of the city finally ended on 21 September 1941 almost 665,000 Russian troops had been captured in the encirclement. Das Reich were exhilarated by the fall of Kiev. Its division had left a trail of devastation in its wake. Across the whole of the front its forces, together with the Wehrmacht, had hammered deep into enemy lines. It seemed that Blitzkrieg had once again been imprinted on the battlefield and there was an aura of invincibility among the men.

Over the next days and weeks that followed the Soviet Army were overwhelmed by the German onslaught. In Army Group Centre it was planned to resume the attack on Moscow, and during the early hours of 30 September 1941, the first phase of the attack on the Russian capital began, codenamed Operation Typhoon. The assault commenced with Panzergruppe II being launched north-eastwards towards Orel, from where it would thrust north behind Yeremenko's Bryansk Front. A few days later Das Reich joined the operation when its units moved with the 10th Panzer Division during the assault on Krichev and Ladishino. For the next two weeks the SS fought a string of bloodthirsty battles, and by the end of October was closing in on Moscow. In spite of strong resistance Das Reich carried on fighting, and after crossing the Istra River it became embroiled in heavy Soviet defensive positions. However, this did not deter the SS from carrying on in spite of the bitter arctic conditions and high casualties, and capturing the town of Istra and the surrounding area. Once again the division pressed on in earnest, but coupled with the cold weather and heavy combat losses, the units steadily became ground down in a battle of attrition.

By the end of November the whole of Army Group Centre's front was becoming progressively stagnated across the freezing plains of the Soviet Union. The Der Führer Regiment had lost huge quantities of men and equipment and the depleted 2nd Battalion assigned its survivors to other parts of the regiment. Deutschland too had suffered immeasurable losses, and its 3rd Battalion had to be broken up and distributed among the other depleted battalions in order for it to survive.

Battered and exhausted, Das Reich and its Wehrmacht counterparts dug in in front of Moscow. Although plans to try to capture the Russian capital before the winter set in had failed, Hitler's policy to hold his tattered frostbitten forces in front of Moscow had in fact saved ground, but at an alarming expenditure in men and material. The Russians, as predicted, finally ran out of power because of the harsh weather, and were unable to achieve any deep penetration into the German lines. This had consequently saved Army Group Centre from complete destruction. Although Hitler was later to say that the battle for Moscow was his finest hour, his army had failed to capture the city, being crucified by Russian winter and by fanatical Soviet resistance. But much of the failure of Operation Typhoon was essentially due to the remarkable Russian recovery and their winter offensive. For the Germans, the battle had completely altered the Wehrmacht from its glorious days in June and July 1941. From now on, it was to carry the scars of Operation Typhoon to its grave. As for the Waffen-SS, it too had been badly mauled by attempts to capture Moscow. The reverberations this caused along the front were so significant that from now on it would always be fire-fighting on the battlefield. It would be hard pressed not only to support Wehrmacht operations that had been stemmed or routed, but would find itself overstretched on the offensive, and later in defensive actions.

The setback on the Eastern Front in late 1941 was so severe militarily that the Waffen-SS and the German army as a whole were doomed to failure. The German objective of capturing Russia by October 1941 had failed. While there was optimism for the following year, and recovery, this would only ever be partial. Russian forces had recovered far quicker and began building up a massive arsenal of weaponry and men to confront the Germans.

As for Das Reich Division, it entered the New Year of 1942 with more than half of its initial strength lost, and could not sustain such high losses for much longer. In total some 8,500 had men had been killed, with another 29,000 missing or wounded.

In spite of the high casualty rate, the division was once again put into action in order to try to smash the growing might of the Soviets. But not even the elite units of the SS could defeat strong Red Army attacks. Its renewed pressure on the German lines throughout February was enough to cause Das Reich further losses in men and equipment. Reluctantly, and to avoid complete annihilation, it was withdrawn from the front to lick its wounds.

The New Year of 1942 brought new hope and confidence to the German Army. Das Reich had made a number of strategic withdrawals in January, but its units were badly depleted. As a consequence late in February the Reich Division was placed on reserve and had its battalions replenished with 3,000 new soldiers.

In March, the SS battle group, or SS-Kampfgruppen, was back in action taking up positions along the River Volga. Once more the SS became heavily embroiled in another offensive which lasted until April. During this period of more or less continuous bloody fighting, often in areas where the SS were dwarfed by the growing scale of Soviet resistance, the Deutschland Regiment was almost annihilated. Luckily for this SS regiment, and indeed the fortunes of the entire Kampfgruppen, the Soviet counteroffensive abated and this consequently permitted German forces along its precarious front line to withdraw and recover.

Two months later, the Das Reich division was transported by train back to Germany to be reorganized and renamed. In November, it became known as the SS-Panzergrenadier-Division Das Reich. Under its new name as the 2nd SS premier division of the Waffen-SS it was given additional armoured support with a Panzer battalion comprising three companies of Pz.Kpfw.IIIs and IVs. The Der Führer Regiment now became fully motorized, and the Reconnaissance Battalion exchanged its motorcycles for Schwimmwagen cars and became 1st Battalion of the newly established Langemarck Regiment.

In November 1942, the Das Reich Division and a handful of other formations moved south and occupied Vichy France. In France Das Reich was once again reorganized and became equipped with a self-propelled gun battalion comprising of three batteries, each possessing seven guns. The Langemarck Regiment was consequently disbanded and some of its men were reassigned to the Panzer Battalion, while 1st Battalion resumed its role as a separate reconnaissance unit.

Now reorganized and fully fitted and replenished, the division received orders that it would once more return to the Eastern Front in Army Group South in the Ukraine and support the drive there.

Das Reich troops at the frontier with the Soviet Union. On 22 June 1941, three German army groups launched their attack against Russia. Included in this massive array of military might were 160,405 soldiers of the Waffen-SS.

Two photographs taken in sequence, showing an infantryman and an NCO, both smiling for the camera with two white puppies on the rear of a Horch cross country vehicle. Note the tactical divisional symbol painted in either white or yellow on the rear of the vehicle. Das Reich's insignia was a rune that resembled a reversed N with a vertical line running down the middle of it. It was known as the 'Wolfsangel', an ancient symbol supposed to protect those who wore it from wolves. Note the letter G painted in white, denoting that the vehicle was attached to Guderian's 2nd Panzergruppe.

A photograph taken from inside a Horch cross country car as it enters a captured Russian town. Most SS soldiers regarded the war with Russia as a holy crusade against Bolshevism and sub-humanity. The SS fought in every theatre of combat except Africa, but it would be here in the vast wastelands of the Soviet Union that they would fight hardest and most fanatically.

A dusty and dishevelled dispatch rider poses for the camera while sitting on his motorcycle during the early phase of the attack into Russia. He is dressed in the familiar rubberized coat.

(**Opposite page**) A motorcycle unit during the summer of 1941. During the first six months of the war in Russia most motorcycle units were converted to reconnaissance duties. However some were still used as couriers.

(**Above**) An artillery observation post and a soldier is using the 6 × 30 Sf.14Z Scherenfernrohr, or scissor binoculars, searching for enemy targets. Each artillery battery had an observation post among the frontline positions.

Entrenched across a hill, these SS troops are preparing to go into action armed with their Karabiner 98K rifles. Tactics in the vast open spaces of Russia were completely different from those used in the west and the Balkans.

The crew of a camouflaged 7.5cm le IG18 gun out in a field with some of the troops hiding behind it for cover. The gun was light and robust and employed a punchy shotgun breech action, but was of limited efficacy against the heavier weapons it faced against the Russians.

Troops queue for food during a pause in their march. One field kitchen could cook 29 gallons of soup or stew for the men, as well as brew 16 gallons of coffee.

(**Above**) An interesting photograph showing a Das Reich column halted on a road somewhere in western Russia. A camouflaged civilian coach has been used to help transport the men to the front. Behind the vehicle are a number of Opel Blitz infantry light trucks.

(**Opposite page**) An SS soldier has taken two rams from a flock to use as a supplement to military rations.

(**Below**) A PaK crew with their 7.5cm le IG18 gun. This weapon was one of the first First World War guns to be issued to the Wehrmacht and later the Waffen-SS.

(**Opposite, above**) Vehicles belonging to Guderian's Panzergruppe are seen advancing along a muddy road. Mud was a formidable foe. The mud produced from a few hours of rain could turn a typical Russian road into a quagmire.

(**Opposite, below**) A long column of vehicles belonging to Das Reich on a muddy road. The Soviet Union proved to be a completely alien environment to the German soldier, and the distances travelled soon proved more of problem than ever imagined. Russia would not only test the endurance of the German soldier's physical and mental endurance, but also his weapons and supplies.

(**Above**) Two soldiers can be seen in a dugout inside a forest. Over the coming weeks soldiers in a number of sectors of the front were compelled to fight against stiffening enemy attacks that were designed not only to hold back the enemy but to deny them any shelter.

Motorcycle with sidecar combination parked in front of a stationary light Horch cross-country vehicle. Although the motorcycle was versatile and built for speed, in Russia, especially during the winter, they performed relatively poorly.

A signalman operating a portable radio. This was the standard radio used at battalion and regimental level. They were carried by a soldier on a specially designed backpack frame and, when connected to each other (upper and lower valves via special cables, could be used on the march.

Winter, early 1942. It is evident in this photograph how unprepared the troops were for winter combat. The majority wear their standard army-issue greatcoat. One is seen wearing the woolen toque, which was a popular winter item during this period of the war. Scarves were sometimes worn with the toque. Two of the soldiers wear the summer Waffen-SS camouflage smocks.

A FlaK crew with their whitewashed 8.8cm FlaK gun. This gun was used in two roles, one against aerial attacks, and the other against ground targets. Here it is being used in the latter role.

To blend in with the terrain this SS squad leader wears a piece of crude white sheeting wrapped around his tunic and on his M35 helmet. In November 1941 large batches of winter clothing were hastily sent to the front-line combat troops.

(**Opposite page**) Two photographs showing a sled containing supplies being towed by animal draught through the snow. There was little respite in the line for these soldiers – if the Red Army let up for a brief period, the sub-zero temperatures did not. As temperatures dropped during November and December 1941 troops improvised on their winter wear using animal skin coats and captured Russian stocks of clothes, which were often lined with fur.

(**Above**) Three soldiers with their commanding officer stand next to their vehicle on an icy road. All across the front both troops and tanks were beginning to grind to a halt in the arctic conditions. The extreme winter of late 1941 had caused the front to stagnate until the spring thaw of 1942, delaying the conquest of Russia by months. The Germans had travelled a vast distance, but had failed to achieve their objective.

(**Above**) A 2cm Flakvierling 38 quadruple self-propelled flak gun mounted on the rear of a Mercedes vehicle during the early winter of 1942. This weapon has clearly been employed in an anti-aircraft role.

(**Opposite, above**) A light MG34 machine gunner lying in the snow with his weapon on its bipod. A well-sited, well-hidden and well-supplied MG34 could hold up an entire attacking regiment.

(**Opposite, below**) An 8.8cm flak gun being readied by its crew for action. This was the most famous German anti-aircraft gun of the Second World War. It was bolted on a cruciform platform with outriggers extended.

In the depths of the Russian winter and a signalman is operating a portable radio (Tornisterfunkgerät or TornFu). This was the standard radio system used at battalion and regimental level.

Commanding officers are about to be driven to a position. It was apparent to German command by late 1941 and early 1942 that the Russians had become more determined than ever to stem the German onslaught by any means possible, from blowing bridges, laying endless anti-tank traps, mining and destroying main roads.

A 2cm Flakvierling 38 quadruple self-propelled flak gun mounted on a platform inside a forest being used as an anti-aircraft weapon. This gun could discharge 1,800 rounds per minute from its four barrels. It had two operators, one who fired the top left and bottom right guns, the other the top right and bottom left guns. The loader could quickly change the magazines while the other continued to fire. Note all the magazines piled next to the weapon.

Soviet PoWs are seen here being led away to a fate that can only be imagined. They pass a staff vehicle that has the letter G painted on the rear, indicating that it belongs to Guderian's Panzergruppe.

(**Opposite, above**) Das Reich troops rest at the side of the road during the spring of 1942. Positioned next to them are two 3.7cm PaK35/36 anti-tank guns. This gun was carried on a two-wheel split-trail carriage of tubular construction with a small, sloped splinter shield. It emerged as the first anti-tank weapon to serve both the Heer and the Waffen-SS, but by this time in the war they were ineffective against well-armoured Soviet tanks.

(**Opposite, below**) Das Reich troops take cover in a field. A Pz.Kpfw.III passes its position. Note the heavily camouflaged 7.5cm le IG light infantry gun. These small, light, highly mobile infantry guns were more than capable of providing troops with vital offensive and defensive fire support, particularly when heavy artillery was unavailable.

(**Above**) A supply vehicle can be seen at a rail hub. Flatbed rail cars can be seen destined for the front lines in Russia. Many thousands of vehicles were transported to the east this way, which not only saved time and effort, but reduced wear and tear. Entire divisions were often moved this way from one part of the front to another.

An interesting photograph showing a shirtless machine gunner with an old First World War Maschinengewehr 08, or MG 08, on a tripod mount in the summer of 1942. The gun used 250-round fabric belts of 7.92mm ammunition, and the belts can be seen around the gunner's torso. The weapon was water-cooled using a jacket around the barrel that held around a gallon of water.

Infantry wearing the winter reversible jackets white side out are seen walking along a trench during the winter of 1942. They are wearing the woolen toque, which was a popular winter item during this period of the war.

Chapter Four

Kharkov and Beyond (1943–44)

Das Reich arrived in the southern sector of the Eastern Front in January 1943. However, by early 1943 fighting tactics on the Eastern Front had changed. Hitler's Waffen-SS premier divisions, of which Das Reich was one, had effectively become the Führer's emergency 'fire brigade', with occasional assistance from a number of less elite SS-Panzergrenadier divisions. Hitler looked to these divisions to blunt the Soviet offensive that had already gained the initiative following the destruction of the 6th Army at Stalingrad. As far as he was concerned, the SS had stood firm in the face of adversity – unlike the regular Heer. In March 1943 Hitler would prove correct when three of his elite divisions, LSSAH, Das Reich, and Totenkopf, of the newly-formed SS-Panzer-Corps, recaptured the city of Kharkov.

Outside Kharkov Das Reich saw extensive fighting against the Soviet 3rd Guards Tank Army. Near the city its forces established a bridgehead between Volokomovka and Kupiansk on the River Oskol. What followed was a bitter and bloody battle for the city of Kharkov along with 1st SS-Panzer-Corps. After the city was captured by the Red Army, Das Reich and other SS units were assigned the task of its recapture.

In early March, the SS-Panzer-Korps, along with Das Reich, attacked Kharkov. By 15 March, the Germans had smashed the last remnants of the Red Army garrison at a tractor factory just east of the city. Das Reich then proceeded to move out of the smouldering city and underwent more reorganization and resupply in order to compensate for the high losses suffered during the Battle of Kharkov.

After stemming the Soviet tide at Kharkov, the SS-Panzer-Corps were prepared to spearhead the German summer offensive on the central sector of the Eastern Front, in the area of Orel and Kursk. This would be the last major offensive operation undertaken by the Germans in the East. What would follow in its wake would be almost two years of bitter, bloody defensive battles with the Waffen-SS being rushed from one disintegrating sector of the front to another, plugging the gaps and fighting to the death in order to slow down the inevitable advance of the Red Army.

In July 1943, combat formations launched what would prove to be the German army's last great offensive on the Eastern Front – against the Kursk salient. The offensive, codenamed Operation Zitadelle, would smash Red Army formations and leave the road to Moscow open. For this daring offensive, the German force was distributed between the Northern and Southern groups and consisted of a total of twenty-two divisions, six of which were Panzer and five Panzergrenadier. Responsibility for the main attack fell to 9th Army in the north, where there were some 335,000 soldiers, 590 tanks and 424 assault guns. In the south, the Germans fielded a force of 349,907 troops, 1,269 tanks and 245 assault guns. Although it was a formidable assembly of firepower, it was in fact facing an even greater enemy coupled with almost impregnable defensive belts. In front of the Soviet defensive fortress stood the premier divisions of the Waffen-SS. In Army Group South these elite soldiers were deployed for action, ready to fight their way through the formidable lines of barbed-wire entanglements, minefields and anti-tank guns. Here, II SS-Panzer-Corps, commanded by SS-Obergruppenführer Paul Hausser, formed part of 4th Panzer-Army. The Corps comprised the three premier Waffen-SS divisions, LSSAH, Das Reich and Totenkopf. The three had a line strength of 390 of the latest tanks and 104 assault guns between them, including 42 of the Army Group's Tigers.

During the days that followed, Das Reich was tasked with guarding the eastern flank of the other two SS divisions, but soon found itself on the defensive against strong Russian resistance. Again and again it fought with all the élan and tenacity of a premier Waffen-SS division, but this did little to stem the rout. Slowly the Germans were ground down in a battle of attrition.

On 15 July, Das Reich made contact with 7th Panzer-Division, but this did nothing to avert what was to become a catastrophe. While Das Reich fanatically contested every foot of ground, the 9th Army was forced to begin a planned withdrawal westwards to avert being encircled and then destroyed. This was followed by the remnants of the II SS-Panzer-Corps, which was now battered and exhausted, being quickly withdrawn out of the Kursk sector to the relative calm of Kharkov.

The Germans, it seemed, had pulled their forces out before they were completely decimated, leaving their hated foe to regain the initiative, not only in the area around Kursk, but also in the east. What would now follow in the aftermath of Kursk would be a series of German withdrawals with the Waffen-SS fighting doggedly from one fixed position to another trying to stabilize the crumbling front lines.

Not deterred by its massive losses, the Soviet Army were determined not to allow the Germans any respite, and continued launching heavy attacks on the River Mius. Even when Das Reich and Totenkopf were rushed to protect Panzer and Wehrmacht forces along the river, they were only able to stop the enemy for short periods while German forces withdrew. Eventually the Waffen-SS could no longer hold the Russians from smashing through, and as a consequence retreated, allowing them to launch a series of massive attacks towards Stalino and Taganrog, and along the northern coast of the Sea of Azov.

By mid-August 1943, the Russians had wrenched open a huge gap in the German lines west of Kursk, once again threatening to retake the important industrial city of Kharkov. Das Reich, Totenkopf and Wiking divisions were immediately thrown into battle to prevent the loss of the city. Although all these combat formations were weakened by the Zitadelle disaster, they were still a formidable fighting force. The city itself had only been recaptured by the Waffen-SS in March 1943, and now it was the Red Army's turn to launch a pincer attack to capture it back again.

Within days of the SS redeployment to Kharkov the Russian 53rd Army driving from north and the 57th Army advancing from the south attacked the city with all their might. Almost immediately the SS troops crashed into action and defended Kharkov with every drop of blood.

On 20 August Totenkopf and the Grossdeutschland divisions joined hands to close the gap west of the city. However, by this stage of the battle both divisions were running out of ammunition and were already relying heavily on artillery to undertake the main burden of defending their positions. The high consumption of ammunition in the last month had put serious strain on all the German combat formations in and around Kharkov. In many units, daily supplies of artillery and tank ammunition were down to half the normal capacity required to sustain a force of such magnitude in a defensive position. And yet, despite these problems, Manstein still thought he might be able to hold Kharkov by using Das Reich in a counterattack. The soldiers of Das Reich were to throw everything they could muster against the Soviets. But when they arrived in the 6th Corps zone of operations, they found that the artillerymen, after firing their last rounds, were abandoning their guns and fighting as infantry.

Fighting around the city was heavy. In just one day, SS anti-tank gunners knocked out nearly 200 Soviet tanks. The Das Reich Panther battalion, which first saw combat on the 22 August, destroyed fifty-three Russian tanks. The next day, just west of Kharkov, a Panther platoon broke up a Russian tank assault, and one Panther destroyed seven tanks. On 24 August, the 6 SS-Panzer-Kompanie, newly supplied with the latest Panzer IVs, battled sixty Russian T-34 tanks between Udy-Bogens and Orkan, just south-west of the city, and knocked out twenty-nine of them. In the ten-day battle around Kharkov the Das Reich division alone scored 463 armoured kills.

Totenkopf and Wiking were equally impressive, and fought a series of skilful duels against numerically superior enemy forces. Again and again they showed their worth in the field of action. In spite of serious losses in men and material, the troops continued fighting with all the ruthlessness and dynamism that made them such an efficient and lethal weapon of war.

Through the later part of August the SS continued to score some outstanding successes in localised combats with Russian armoured units. However, with acute shortages in men and equipment the situation deteriorated day by day. Despite frantic calls from commanders appealing for the evacuation of the city, Hitler sent out an order that Kharkov be held under all circumstances and demanded the most severe measures against any units that failed to execute their assigned missions. Both Wehrmacht and Waffen-SS units were forced to undertake their Führer's futile exercise of holding Kharkov to grim death.

As the situation deteriorated, Hitler became increasingly worried that another Stalingrad would develop. By early September he grudgingly decided to allow the troops to pull out of the doomed city, and the Waffen-SS withdrew towards the River Dnieper. Here the SS managed to halt the Russian advance, allowing Manstein's forces to retreat and redeploy. Totenkopf, Das Reich and Grossdeutschland had helped avert a major disaster and now retired to the western bank of the river.

Some 68 German divisions – 1,250,000 men and over 2,000 tanks of Army Group South – were tasked with holding the river line at all costs. Opposing them was a Red Army almost double in size, with plenty of reserves of fresh men and equipment. Manstein was well aware that his army group could no longer hold the Donets Line.

North along the River Dnieper soldiers of Das Reich had meanwhile been trying to prevent enemy forces from consolidating control areas west of the river. SS troopers had been battling Red Army forces through late September and October trying to stop the Russians establishing a bridgehead. The Der Führer regiment had seized the town of Grebeni, but at great cost. Only 500 soldiers were left in its ranks. Undaunted, Das Reich continued to fight a number of inconclusive battles in the region, which saw its regiments and battalions become further depleted.

Throughout the weeks that ominously followed, the German front lines were pulled farther westwards with Das Reich defending, attacking and counter-attacking as the situation demanded. A number of the battles that were fought and won in this sector of the front were owed to the efforts of the SS, but they came with a high price in blood. While Das Reich had fought well and with distinction to prevent the Russians from marching across western Ukraine, it had been unrelenting and proved to be more than it could endure. Consequently, by December 1943, it was no longer capable of carrying out the tasks given to a full-strength division, and orders were issued to create a Kampfgruppe from the units still fit for action.

On 17 December, the Panzer Kampfgruppe was formed out of Panzergrenadier-Regiment Das Reich. The Kampfgruppe consisted of 1st Battalion Deutschland and 2nd Battalion Der Führer Regiments. Two companies constituted the Panzer-Battalion Das Reich, and also on strength were the reconnaissance battalion, artillery, Nebelwerfers, pioneers, a heavy infantry gun company and two self-propelled gun companies. The bulk of Kampfgruppe Das Reich, as it was now called, would remain on the Eastern Front while the remaining elements returned to Germany for a refit.

In January 1944, Das Reich was rushed to what became known as the Korsun Pocket, where more than 35,000 Wehrmacht troops became encircled and then consequently trapped. The SS were determined to wrench open the pocket and allow as many troops as possible to break free. As a result of this sacrifice, Das Reich suffered massive losses, but enabled some 33,000 German troops to escape with their lives. Depleted and under strength in both men and armour, the division, apart from a Kampfgruppe under the command of SS-Oberführer Heinz Lammerding, was pulled out of the Eastern Front in April 1944 and sent to France for recuperation.

At the gates of Kharkov in March 1943 and a VW Type 166 Schwimmwagen can be seen on a road. This vehicle was more than likely used outside Kharkov when Das Reich saw extensive fighting against the Soviet 3rd Guards tank army. It was near the city where its forces maintained a bridgehead between Volokomovka and Kupiansk on the River Oskol. Interestingly, the parked Schwimmwagen are from an LSSAH reconnaissance battalion. This is one of the platoons of the motorized companies, which in 1942 had exchanged motorcycles for light, mobile cars.

Panzergrenadier of Das Reich have hitched a lift onboard a Pz.Kpfw.III as it enters the city of Kharkov during intensive action to capture the city. Note the Das Reich divisional insignia painted in yellow on the rear of the tank.

(**Opposite, above**) Das Reich Panzergrenadier during the battle for Kharkov. An MG42 can be seen slung over the shoulder of one soldier. They are all wearing their Waffen-SS reversible padded jackets grey side out. The SS units involved in the fighting inside the city were fully motorized and troops did not carry a full set of field equipment.

(**Opposite, below**) A Das Reich MG42 machine gunner with his weapon on its bipod aims towards wasteland during intensive action for Kharkov. This battle was part of the Donets campaign and its objective was for a massive German counterstrike using premier SS divisions to recapture the cities of Kharkov and Belgorod.

(**Above**) A photograph showing an Unterscharführer of the SS-Panzercorps in Kharkov. He is armed with an MP40 and his battledress consists of winter reversible trousers, field grey 'parka' fur jacket and felt boots.

(**Above**) Troops trying to push a vehicle through the mud. The bad road system in the east was a hindrance to the Germans throughout the war.

(**Opposite page**) SS infantry unloading postbags. Receiving mail was important for the morale of frontline soldiers.

(**Below**) Waffen-SS soldiers on the march during the early phase of the battle of Kursk in July 1943. In front of the Soviet defensive fortress at Kursk stood the elite of all the German combat formations. The professionalism and technical ability of the SS were second to none. These SS troops wear their familiar SS camouflage smocks.

Two photographs showing infantry pushing forward during the Kursk offensive. During the first day of the attack, Heer and Waffen-SS soldiers progressed well against stiff Red Army resistance. However, the first line of Russian defence seemed almost impossible to break through.

Das Reich troops on the move. Behind them is a variety of armoured vehicles spread out across a field in the Kursk salient. The initial phase of the fighting at Kursk had been very costly to the Russians, but in a tactical and operational sense it achieved its objectives. During the days that followed, the Red Army began to deprive the SS of its tactical advantage.

Nebeltruppen can be seen loading Nebelwerfer 41 rockets into a carrier for transportation. The shells weighed 34kg and could be projected over a range of 7,000 metres. When fired, the projectiles screamed through the air, terrifying the enemy. Because it was dangerous for the crew to remain close to the launcher while the piece was being fired, it was fired remotely using an electrical detonator attached to a cable, which ran to the piece.

A StuG.III moves along in a field supporting the infantry. By the summer of 1943 the StuG.III had become a popular assault gun on the battlefield. The vehicles had initially provided crucial mobile fire support to the infantry and also proved their worth as anti-tank weapons. But at Kursk they were primarily used as an anti-tank weapon, thus depriving the infantry of vital fire support.

A Tiger tank belonging to Das Reich II SS Panzer-Korps rolls forward into action with SS troops on foot. SS Panzer and Panzergrenadier divisions had become known as the 'fire brigade' of the Third Reich. Wherever they were committed to battle, they attacked. Sometimes the outcome was successful, but there were many failures too.

Troops and vehicles advance towards strong Red Army fortifications during the early part of the Kursk offensive. Note how they are purposely spaced apart in order to reduce casualties.

An MG gun troop was normally a three-man squad as in this photograph, but due to the high casualty rates suffered on the eastern front they were commonly reduced to two, but still highly effective. Although successful in an offensive role, the MG42 was equally good in a defensive role, proving its worth time and again.

Das Reich soldiers advance through a sunflower field. Despite a number of successful engagements by the Waffen-SS in the Kursk salient the Red Army remained strong and was rapidly developing into a skilful army with enormous quantities of men and material.

Three photographs taken in sequence showing Das Reich soldiers aiding an injured Soviet tank man. Behind them a knocked-out T34 can be seen. They wear the 'plane tree' pattern camouflage helmet cover and a 'palm' pattern camouflage smock.

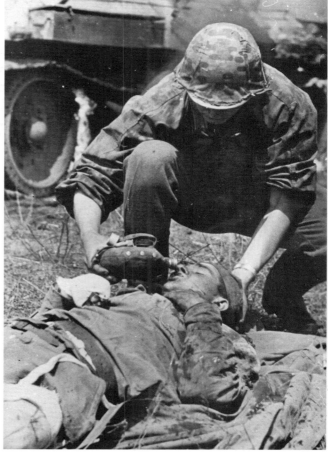

(**Opposite page**) In a trench and troops can be seen resting before going back into action. Note the radio man wearing his headset with the Torn.Fu.b1 pack radio.

(**Above**) A MG troop hiding in overgrowth during Kursk. This would be the last major offensive operation undertaken by the Germans in the east. What would follow would be almost two years of bitter, bloody defensive battles with the Waffen-SS being rushed to one disintegrating sector of the front to another, plugging the gaps and fighting to the death to slow down the inevitable advance of the Red Army.

(**Left**) A soldier confers with his commanding officer. In front of them, troops have dug into the side of a hill, which offered them some protection from enemy fire.

A decorated SS tank man is congratulated by his commanding officer in the summer of 1943.

Commanding officers belonging to the Deutschland regiment can be seen surveying the battlefield from their command vehicle.

Two stationary late Pz.Kpfw.IIIs can be seen in a field. One of the tanks is a command vehicle and has been fitted out with long-range radio antennae. Commanding officers can be seen conversing, one holding a map board.

Pz.Kpfw.IVs can be seen in field in the summer of 1943. Initially the Panzer IV was designed as an infantry support tank, but soon proved to be so diverse and effective that it earned a unique tactical role on the battlefield. The Panzer IV was a credit to the Panzer divisions it served and was the only Panzer to stay in production throughout the war. They were also used by the premier SS divisions.

SS troops in a defensive position. A typical strongpoint deployed along the German front comprised mainly light and heavy MG34 and MG42 machine guns, anti-tank rifles, sappers equipped with various explosives, infantry guns, anti-tank artillery, and occasionally a self-propelled gun.

A Waffen-SS crew with their 7.5cm PaK40 during a fire mission. The PaK40 was a popular weapon in the Heer and the Waffen-SS and there were never enough of them.

SS infantry take cover along a road while a late variant StuG.III Ausf.G passes by.

An assault gun has become stuck in muddy water and a halftrack is attempting to pull it out of the mire using the StuG's tow cables.

A variety of armoured vehicles including a Pz.Kpfw.IV, Panther V, and Sd.Kfz.251 halftrack can be seen spread out across snowy terrain in the early winter of 1944.

In the winter of 1944 and an SS crew can be seen with their 7.5cm PaK40. This PaK gun proved its worth in Russia and was more than capable of disabling heavy Soviet tanks.

Two photographs showing
Nebelwerfer 41s in a field
before and during a fire
mission. The Nebelwerfer 41
was equipped with six barrels,
each firing a 34kg 150mm
Wurfgranate 41 (rocket shell)
to a range of approximately
6,800 meters. Along the
German front the Nebelwerfer
was used extensively and
caused high losses in the
Russian lines.

(**Above**) SS and Heer troops on the march during the autumn of 1944. An Sd.Kfz.251 halftrack personnel carrier can be seen carrying Panzergrenadiers. These vehicles were used extensively during the latter half of the war to transport Panzergrenadiers to the forward edge of the battlefield. Despite their armour, they could keep up with the fast-moving spearheads.

(**Opposite page**) Committed opposition to the SS had led to the premier divisions obtaining more infantry support weapons, notably assault guns from the artillery. Since 1941 Das Reich had increased its numbers of assault gun batteries to high levels to help deal with the threat on the Eastern Front. Here in this photograph one of Das Reich's StuG.IIIs is being loaded onto a railway flatbed for transportation to the front.

(**Above, left**) A well concealed Sd.Kfz.251 halftrack. Armoured vehicles and halftrack personnel carriers not only provided the mobility that was crucial to success on the battlefield, but they also became synonymous with the fighting skill of the Waffen-SS.

(**Above, right**) Troops pause in the march. Next to a well camouflaged vehicle soldiers cook some food over a fire. They were issued a march ration of sausage, cheese, dried bread, coffee, and sugar in paper bags. Where they could, they would supplement their rations by finding animals to cook.

(**Opposite, above**) Out in the field and a Das Reich gun crew can be seen with its 7.5cm le IG18 light infantry artillery piece. This weapon was used in direct infantry support. It was versatile in combat and the crew often aggressively positioned it, meaning the piece was regularly exposed on the battlefield. A typical infantry regiment controlled three infantry battalions and an infantry gun company with six 7.5cm le IG18s. This was reduced as the war progressed.

(**Opposite, below**) A Das Reich soldier is seen laying a Tellermine 43. This mine was a steel-cased anti-tank blast mine. It was armed by removing the pressure plate, screwing a fuse into the fuse well, then screwing the pressure plate back on again, as seen in this photograph. Millions of these mines were laid across Russia and Poland during the last two years of the war.

Chapter Five

End Game
(1944–45)

While Das Reich was recuperating in the south of France during the summer of 1944, the division received news of the Allied invasion in northern France on 6 June 1944. Two days later some 15,000 soldiers and 209 Panzers and self-propelled guns began pulling out of the town of Montauban to begin an arduous march across 450 miles of French countryside towards the shores of Normandy.

On their way they were harassed by the French Resistance and agents of the Allied Special Forces. Consequently, what followed was a series of savage reprisals that were some of the most appalling atrocities committed in the Second World War.

In the tiny hamlet of Groslejac, Das Reich soldiers killed a number of civilians. A hotel was hit by artillery fire. As it burst into flames, the terrified inhabitants tried to escape through the front door, only to be shot by machine guns as they emerged.

In the town of Tulle, where resistance fighters killed forty soldiers, the SS murdered ninety-nine of its inhabitants, all of whom were hanged from the street lamp posts.

On the afternoon of 10 June the population of the town of Oradour-sur-Glane were rounded up and brutally murdered, the SS killing and burning to death women, children and old people.

Resistance against the division ended at Bellac, near Poitiers. Partisan warfare had not been extinguished in the area, but the resistance had decided not to attempt any more attacks due to the SS reprisals. Instead, RAF bombing caused considerable damage in the Loire region hampering daylight movement by Das Reich. By the time the division arrived in the Normandy sector between 15 and 30 June, it was in bad shape and required a few days to regroup before going into action.

The division was put into the battle line on 10 July and on 4 August took part in a counter-offensive from Vire towards Avranches called Operation Lüttich. However, due to strong Allied air power the SS positions were mercilessly bombed and the operation was halted. By the end of August Das Reich had sustained massive losses in men and equipment, and what was left from the Normandy campaign limped across the Seine. The US 2nd Armoured Division then encircled elements of Das Reich, including most of the 17th SS Panzergrenadier Division Götz von Berlichingen, around Roncey. By September 1944 Das Reich had lost 2,650 men along with fourteen 7.5cm PaK guns, thirty-seven artillery pieces, an assault gun and a Panther tank with two other tanks in the repair shop.

All the remained of Das Reich was now 450 men and 15 tanks. They pulled back behind the West Wall fortification in France to the area of Schnee Eifel.

Three months later the division was once again embroiled in heavy combat, this time in the Ardennes. The codename for this historic offensive was 'Wacht am Rhein' (Watch on the Rhine) and it was planned to begin in the early morning of 16 December 1944.

Initially Das Reich's advance through the Ardennes went well coming within sight of the River Meuse. However there the division was halted, and then slowly smashed by fierce Allied counter-attacks. Before it was completely annihilated it was pulled out and transferred to Germany for another refit. From here Das Reich was ordered to take part in the last German offensive of the war, to break the siege around Budapest.

When Das Reich arrived in Hungary in January 1945 it was not the same mighty SS combat formation that had fought previously in the east. In spite of being low in manpower and armour it fought doggedly and defended its ground, but slowly and systematically it was engulfed by superior Soviet forces. By 2 April, the Russians had reached Lake Neusiedler on the border between Hungary and Austria, and two days later the last German defenders had been finally driven out of Hungary. Of the Waffen-SS divisions that had fought in Hungary, the bulk of them withdrew into Austria to defend Vienna. The LSSAH and Das Reich were put into the line to defend Vienna, before withdrawing into the city and becoming involved in bitter fighting. However, by 13 April, the Red Army marched into the city. By this period of the war, the bulk of the premier Waffen-SS divisions were carrying out a fighting withdrawal through Hungary and Austria. In May, scattered into separate battle groups, Das Reich disbanded along with all the other Waffen-SS formations. Although Das Reich had all but been destroyed, in the eyes of the SS soldiers that marched into captivity, they had laid down their arms in the sound knowledge that no military formation in history had achieved more. They had battled across half of Russia, had shown their skill and endurance at Kursk and Kharkov, and gone on to protect the withdrawal of the rest of the German Army to the very gates of Berlin and beyond.

Two photographs showing Pz.Kpfs.IVs and a Tiger tank in the winter of 1944. Waffen-SS tank crews dominated the battlefields of the latter half of the war. But although they destroyed thousands of enemy tanks, they never had the numbers to change the course of the war.

Nebelwerfer 41s during a fire mission in a field.

(**Above**) A 7.5cm PaK40 crew during a fire mission. In 1944 the PaK40 was still widely used in both the Heer and Waffen-SS with deadly effect.

(**Opposite, above**) SS men armed with an with MP40 of the SS Panzer-Korps posing for the camera after winning the *Eisernes Kreuz*. Note the Sd.Kfz.251 behind the soldier with the name 'Bussard' painted on the side in white.

(**Opposite, below**) Units of Das Reich on the move on flatbed railway cars. This was one of the quickest methods for troop movement. Moving during the day was constantly hampered by aerial attacks, and as a result many units often moved by train at night. Note the camouflage on the vehicles.

(**Above**) Commanding officers take cover in what appears to be a bomb crater during operations in the Normandy sector in July 1944. The Allies mercilessly bombed positions and by the end of August Das Reich had sustained massive losses in men and equipment. What was left from the Normandy campaign limped back across the Seine.

(**Opposite page**) A signals post in the Normandy sector in the summer of 1944. Even by this late period of the war rapid transmission of orders via radio and the fast action taken in response to them were the keys to the success of the Waffen-SS maintaining its position cohesively on the front line. The equipment issued to the signals units varied from field telephone sets, to ten-line subscriber networks and teleprinters, as well as transmitters and receivers.

(**Above**) A section leader or SS-Unterscharführer on the right can be seen with an SS stormtrooper (or SS-Sturmmann) during Das Reich's retreat across northern France in the summer of 1944.

(**Opposite page**) Two photographs showing SS troops after their regroup in September or October 1944. Following the Normandy campaign, what was left of Das Reich, some 450 men and 15 tanks, pulled back behind the West Wall fortification in France where it rested in the area of Schnee Eifel before being sent back to the west again later that year.

Infantry trying to remove a vehicle that has become stuck in mud in Hungary in January 1945. By now Das Reich was not the same mighty SS combat formation that had fought previously in the east, but it never ceased to fight doggedly to defend its ground.

An Sd.kfz.251 halftrack towing a supply vehicle by a river in Hungary in early 1945.

Fuel had become scarce by early 1945. Here StuG.IIIs are being refuelled from a mobile fuel supply vehicle in Hungary. In spite of the shortages, assault guns and self-propelled guns proved indispensable to the Waffen-SS on the Eastern Front.

A 5cm PaK 38 crew near a road during operations in early 1945. Fighting in Hungary was bitter, and both Heer and Waffen-SS anti-tank units fought almost continuously to try to hold back the advancing Red Army.

An SS Flak gun mounted on top of a vehicle near a road in early 1945. By 1944, mechanized formations were well equipped with flak guns. There were motorized flak battalions, with divisions being furnished with additional anti-aircraft platoons and companies in the Panzergrenadier, Panzer and artillery regiments. This flak gun was a formidable weapon more than capable of combating both low-flying aircraft and ground targets.

Das Reich troops run across a road towards a burning Russian tank. Throughout the defensive fighting on the Eastern Front soldiers of the Waffen-SS fought courageously and continued to battle from one receding front to another.

The price of winning the war in the East. A dead Soviet anti-tank gunner lies next to his anti-tank gun in April 1945.

Appendix

Order of battle

SS-Division Verfügungstruppe, 1939–41

SS.VT-Standarte Der Führer
SS.VT-Standarte Deutschland
SS.VT-Standarte Germania
SS.VT-Artillerie-Standarte
SS.VT-Artillerie-Standarte
SS.VT-Aufklärung-Abteilung
SS.VT-Panzerjäger Bataillon
SS.VT-Flak-Abteilung
SS.VT-Pioneer-Abteilung
SS.VT-Nachrichten-Abteilung
SS.VT-Panzerabwehr-Abteilung
SS.VT-Flak-Abteilung
SS-Ersatz-Abteilung

SS Division Das Reich, 1941–2

SS-Infanterie Regiment Deutschland
I. Battalion, companies 1 to 8
III. Battalion, companies 9 to 16

SS-Infanterie Regiment Der Führer

Leichte Infanterie Kolonne
II. Battalion, companies 5 to 8
III. Battalion, companies 9 to 16

SS Infanterie Regiment 11 (formerly
    SS-Totenkopf-Standarte 11)

Leichte Infanterie Kolonne
I. Battalion, companies 1 to 4
II. Battalion, companies 5 to 8

III. Battalion, companies 9 to 16

Leichte Infanterie Kolonne

Artillerie Regiment
I. Abteilung, batteries 1 to 3
II. Abteilung, batteries 4 to 6
III. Abteilung, batteries 7 to 9
IV. Abteilung, batteries 13 to 15

Sturmgeschütz Batterie Messbatterie
Krad Schützen Bataillon, companies 1 to 5
Aufklärungs Abteilung, companies 1 to 3
Leichte Aufklärungskolonne
Panzerjäger Abteilung, companies 1 to 3
Pionier Abteilung, companies 1 to 3
Brückenkolonne
Leichte Pionier Kolonne
Nachrichten Abteilung, companies 1 and 2
Leichte Nachrichten Kolonne
Wirtschafts Bataillon
Verpflegungsamt
Bäckerie Kompanie
Schlachterie Kompanie
Nachschubdienste
Kraftwagenkolonne 1 to 15
Nachschubkompanie Instandsetzungsdienst
Werkstattkompanie 1 to 3
Ersatz Kolonne

Sanitätsabteilung – Feldlazarett
Sanitätskompanie 1 and 2
Krankenkraftwagenzug 1 to 3

SS Panzergrenadier Division Das Reich, 1942–3

SS Panzergrenadier Regiment
   Deutschland
I. Battalion, companies 1 to 4
II. Battalion, companies 5 to 8
III. Battalion, companies 9 to 13

SS Panzergrenadier Regiment Der Führer
I. Battalion, companies 1 to 4
II. Battalion, companies 5 to 8
III. Battalion, companies 9 to 13

Artillerie Regiment
I. Abteilung, batteries 1 to 3
II. Abteilung, batteries 4 to 6
III. Abteilung, batteries 7 to 9
IV. Abteilung, batteries 10 to 12

Kradschützen Bataillon Langemarck,
   companies 1 to 4

Panzer Regiment
I. Abteilung, companies 1 to 3
II. Abteilung, companies 4 to 6
Schwere Panzer Kompanie
Panzer Pionier Kompanie
Panzer Werkstatt Kompanie
Leichte Panzer Kolonne 1 and 2
Sturmgeschütz Abteilung,
   batteries 1 to 3
Aufklärungs Abteilung, companies 1 to 3
Leichte Aufklärungskolonne
Panzerjäger Abteilung, companies 1 to 3
Flak Abteilung, batteries 1 to 5
Leichte Artillerie Kolonne
Pionier Abteilung, companies 1 to 3
Brückenkolonne
Leichte Pionier Kolonne
Nachrichten Abteilung,
   companies 1 and 2
Leichte Nachrichten Kolonne

Wirtschafts Bataillon
Verpflegungsamt
Bäckerie Kompanie
Schlachterie Kompanie
Nachschubdienste
Kraftwagenkolonne 1 to 15
Nachschubkompanie
Waffen Werkstattkompanie
Instandsetzungsdienst
Werkstattkompanie 1 to 3
Ersatz Kolonne

Sanitätsabteilung – Feldlazarett
Sanitätskompanie 1 and 2
Krankenkraftwagenzug 1 to 3

Stabskompanie
Feldgendarmerie Kompanie
Feldpostamt
Kriegsberichter Kompanie

SS Panzer Division Das Reich, 1943–5

SS-Panzer Regiment 2
I. Abteilung, companies 1 to 3
II. Abteilung, companies 4 to 6

SS Panzergrenadier Regiment Deutschland
I. Battalion, companies 1 to 4
II. Battalion, companies 5 to 8
III. Battalion, companies 9 to 13

SS Panzergrenadier Regiment Der Führer
I. Battalion, companies 1 to 4
II. Battalion, companies 5 to 8
III. Battalion, companies 9 to 13

SS-Panzer Artillerie Regiment 2
I. Abteilung, batteries 1 to 3
II. Abteilung, batteries 4 to 6
III. Abteilung, batteries 7 to 9
IV. Abteilung, batteries 10 to 12

SS-Kradschützen Bataillon 2,
    companies 1 to 5
SS-Sturmgeschütz Abteilung 2,
    batteries 1 to 3
SS-Aufklarungs Abteilung 2,
    companies 1 to 3
Leichte Aufklärungskolonne
SS-Panzerjäger Abteilung 2,
    companies 1 to 3
SS-Flak Abteilung 2, batteries 1 to 5
Leichte Artillerie Kolonne
SS-Panzer Pionier Abteilung 2,
    companies 1 to 3
Brückenkolonne Leichte Pionier Kolonne
SS-Nachrichten Abteilung 2,
    companies 1 and 2
Leichte Nachrichten Kolonne
SS-Wirtschafts Bataillon 2

Verpflegungsamt
Bäckerie Kompanie
Schlachterie Kompanie
SS-Nachschubdienste 2
Kraftwagenkolonne 1 to 15
Nachschubkompanie
Waffen Werkstattkompanie
SS-Instandsetzungsdienst
Werkstattkompanie 1 to 3
Ersatz Kolonne

SS-Sanitätsabteilung – Feldlazarett
Sanitatskompanie 1 and 2
Krankenkraftwagenzug 1 to 3

Stabskompanie
Feldgendarmerie Truppe
Feldpostamt
SS-Kriegsberichter Zug 2